Nell Hill's
Christmas at Home

Text by Mary Caldwell

Photography by Bryan E. McCay

Nell Hill's
Christmas at Home

Mary Carol Garrity

Andrews McMeel
Publishing

Kansas City

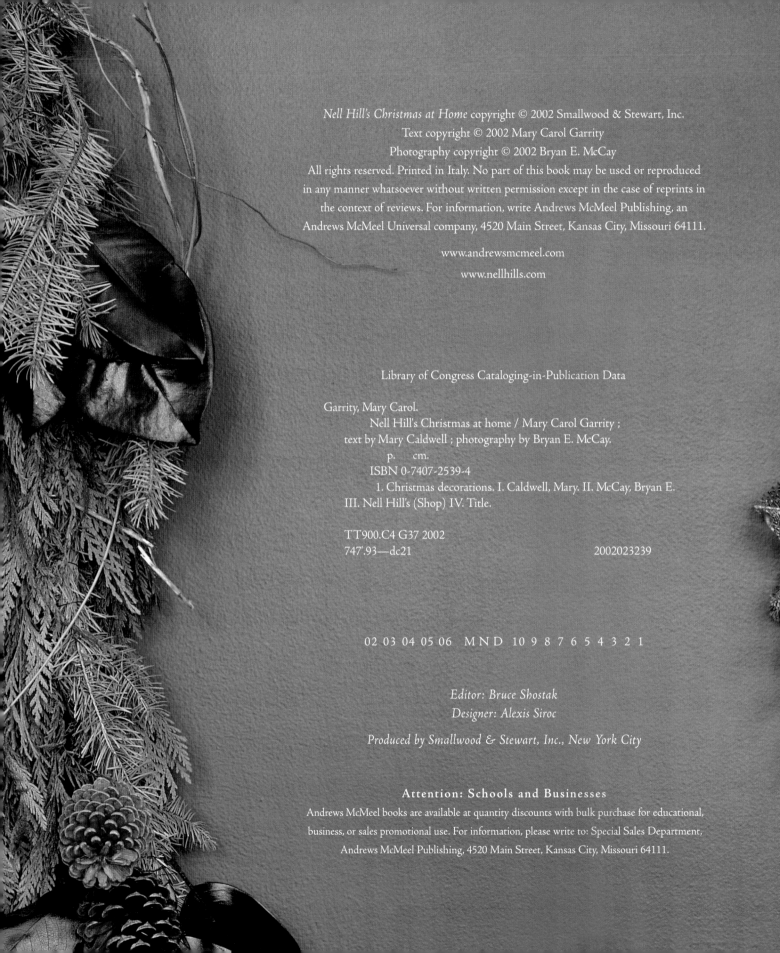

www.andrewsmcmeel.com

www.nellhills.com

Library of Congress Cataloging-in-Publication Data

Garrity, Mary Carol.
   Nell Hill's Christmas at home / Mary Carol Garrity ;
text by Mary Caldwell ; photography by Bryan E. McCay.
      p.   cm.
   ISBN 0-7407-2539-4
      1. Christmas decorations. I. Caldwell, Mary. II. McCay, Bryan E.
III. Nell Hill's (Shop) IV. Title.

TT900.C4 G37 2002
747'.93—dc21   2002023239

02 03 04 05 06 M N D 10 9 8 7 6 5 4 3 2 1

Editor: Bruce Shostak
Designer: Alexis Siroc

Produced by Smallwood & Stewart, Inc., New York City

Attention: Schools and Businesses

Andrews McMeel books are available at quantity discounts with bulk purchase for educational,
business, or sales promotional use. For information, please write to: Special Sales Department,
Andrews McMeel Publishing, 4520 Main Street, Kansas City, Missouri 64111.

To my sister,
Judith Karen Diebolt,
who makes all
my holidays happy.

chapter 1

Welcome Inside

16

chapter 2

Ornaments, Ornaments

34

chapter 3

Woodland Wonder

52

chapter 4

Illuminations

72

chapter 5

Settings for Guests

88

chapter 6

Little Surprises

104

Introduction

Before the dishes from Thanksgiving dinner are cleared,

I've already had Christmas in my two shops,

Nell Hill's and G. Diebolts, in Atchison, Kansas.

But I'm ready — so ready — to bring the holiday home.

When we introduce Christmas at the shops (as early

as August), visitors begin to share their holiday stories

with us. We, too, have our own family traditions. . . .

In Nell Hill's Christmas at Home,

we take a good, long, often surprising look at the holidays. I grew up in a home where every Christmas season was filled with joy. I still love Christmas. All of us who work at the stores, which during the holidays can be more than fifty, have favorite ideas from our families.

How you create a holiday mood in your own home depends on what makes you happy. Do you adore over-the-top rooms that shout "Joy to the World!" from every corner? Are you drawn to a subtle, reverent approach? Perhaps you're like so many of us and enjoy a bit of both: some glamorous clamor, some tranquility.

It's fun to pull out all the stops and completely transform the mood of a setting. The dining room takes naturally to a theatrical atmosphere as guests come in to see and be seen for an evening. I've always been drawn to the winter forest, so I created one in my own dining room (that's it on page 12, and on page 13 before I got busy). The decorations overhead,

on the walls, and layered on the dining table give the mood of an enchanted woodland under a starry sky. In other spots a simple touch is best. One couple I know create the most divine holiday decorations on their living room mantel, and that's it — the rest of the room carries on its everyday life through the season.

To my mind, Christmas decorating isn't an either/or proposition. I don't want to pack away all the things I love looking at during the rest of the year just because the calendar says December. Instead, it's fun to find a little twist that allows favorite objects to take on an integral part of the holiday mood.

It's the most wonderful time of the year — to show love and appreciation. In *Nell Hill's Christmas at Home,* you'll find gifts grand and tiny but always thoughtful — sweet containers for presents, clever places to hide them, and lovely ways to welcome guests and share the season's joy.

Mary Carol

I love to
transform
my favorite
everyday
pieces.

Welcome
Inside

Did you ever go for a car drive

to look at the fantasy of outdoor decorations for the Christmas season? I've always loved the exuberance of those chaotic yards, especially in the midst of a harsh midwestern winter. When I was a child, no display could be over the top: Santa popping into a chimney was the best! The quiet house with a candle in each window and a restrained wreath on the door? To me, it was not exactly enthralling.

Outdoor holiday decorations cheer anybody passing by and I get a lift, too, coming back to a merry house after a day at work (I keep lights on automatic timers to go on before dusk). Just like rooms inside, facades and gardens can take on almost any personality. My friends Merrilee and Mike Bozzoli have one of those old-fashioned front porches so many people dream about. Their easy, yet jolly, decorating relies on lots of greenery; great garlands of it are swagged through porch railings and looped into place partway up the columns

(pages 16–17). The grand urns flanking the walkway are year-round pots for evergreen trees and ivy; come Christmas, they're ready-made decorations. Merrilee and Mike would probably sell the house before they tacked ornaments on these evergreens.

My own front door (opposite) is more formal, but I love greens in abundance — and no tight, dainty garlands for me either. I prefer the freewheeling fullness of greenery spiraling gaily around the columns, as if it's been twisted and tangled by some mischievous forest sprite. Now I can't imagine a front door at Christmas without a wreath and I put a wreath in each window, but I don't stop there. Evergreen wreaths look pretty laid on their sides, perhaps to corral lanterns. When a wreath is placed on top of an urn (page 20), a voluptuous outline results. Then a humble bundle of winter-bare branches becomes a showy bouquet just waiting for some fat snowflakes to arrive.

Home for the Holidays

So many books say they're about simple ways to

transform a home into a celebration of the season.

This one isn't! I'm interested in anything that's fun and

anything that's beautiful, whether it's easy or a little

more ambitious. And I'm not bound by tradition;

just because I did it one way last time doesn't mean

I have to repeat it over and over. That would be

like getting the same present every year!

The candle in the window has long been a signal of welcome. On a sill (above), vintage glass stemware elevates a quartet of votive candles so they peek out above the sash. The painted wall pocket that holds fresh flowers on my back porch in summer is promoted to the front door (opposite) for the holidays. Here it might boast the day's Christmas cards, a couple sprigs of holly, or a handful of candy canes.

Send a warm greeting before guests
even step through the front door.

gestures of hospitality

1 | 2

As I breeze through the entry, I let a touch or two convey holiday spirit there.

In the midwest, the winter landscape can be dreary, especially when there's no fresh snow. It's *rejuvenating* to have live, flowering plants around. *Paper-whites* are fun because they grow and bloom so quickly.

A *tumble* of dried hydrangeas, moss, and taffeta ribbon cascades over a front-hall wardrobe, *high enough* so that it won't get in the way of the season's overcoat-scarf-boot activity.

This bronze *goddess* considers her holiday ornament a beacon. Evergreen conceals a length of fishing line that holds the glass securely. Her laurel crown? For the holidays, it becomes a *wreath*.

As an
aside

A hall table is a handy spot for an evolving arrangement of cards and holiday
bits and pieces. Set out a cachepot to hold keys and gloves.

❀ When they're stacked under a cloche, humble pinecones become
   a little study in nature. The cloche, ornament, and tumbler holding
   candy canes harmonize because all three are glass.

❀ A trio of mismatched vintage toast racks boasts holiday cards and
   awaits greetings from the daily mail.

❀ Placing pieces at different heights enlivens any arrangement.
   Footed cake plates, overturned bowls, and stacks of books all make
   handy pedestals.

❀ A still-life doesn't have to be symmetrical; in fact it's got more
   visual energy if it's slightly off-guard. A case in point: the paper-
   whites at a corner of the table are fine without a counterbalance.

An impressive decoration needn't be an exhaustive one, as my friends Donna and Tim Zimmer demonstrate at their historic home here in Atchison. They want something for the holidays that will stand up to the entry's rich red walls and immense wooden staircase without creating visual cacophony. They don't swag garlands up around the banister; instead they play up the newel post with a fabulous spray that includes wide ribbons and slender, arching pheasant plumes. By the same measure, delicate ornaments would have looked silly on the handsome hall tree; instead it gets a lush frame of fresh greenery, ribbons, feathers, and super-size glass balls.

A bold idea can be more jovial than yards of garland or electric lights.

W hen it comes to Christmas, I can't restrain myself around the fire-place; I am totally extravagant. I start by covering the mantel itself with a sheet of plywood that's been cut to fit; this protects it from sap and nails. I adore great big boughs, which I staple directly to the board. Don't be afraid

Play up your hearth's ability to captivate.

to mix in imitation greens; their quality has improved dramatically and they are appropriate on a warm mantel, where real evergreens quickly lose their needles. I take down the painting that's usually above the fireplace and I hang a wreath on the existing hook, working with a spray of greenery that's wrapped around fishing line. Finally, I mist, mist, mist the greens — several times a day — to keep them fresh.

Invisible but potent decorating: Let scent intensify the holiday mood.

I think aroma is the most powerful way to evoke memories. The fragrance of fresh balsam instantly transports me back to childhood and the magic of my earliest holidays. In my mother's kitchen, Christmas baking created luscious aromas. Now, if there's not enough time to bake before guests arrive, I'll perk coffee, mull cider, or simmer cinnamon and sweet spices in water. Aromatic candles, fresh flowers, even the fragrance of chocolate — all heighten the holiday atmosphere; it's only a matter of orchestrating them to create harmony, not a war of scents. I have an abiding rule that every room in the house must have the scent of Christmas.

fragrance

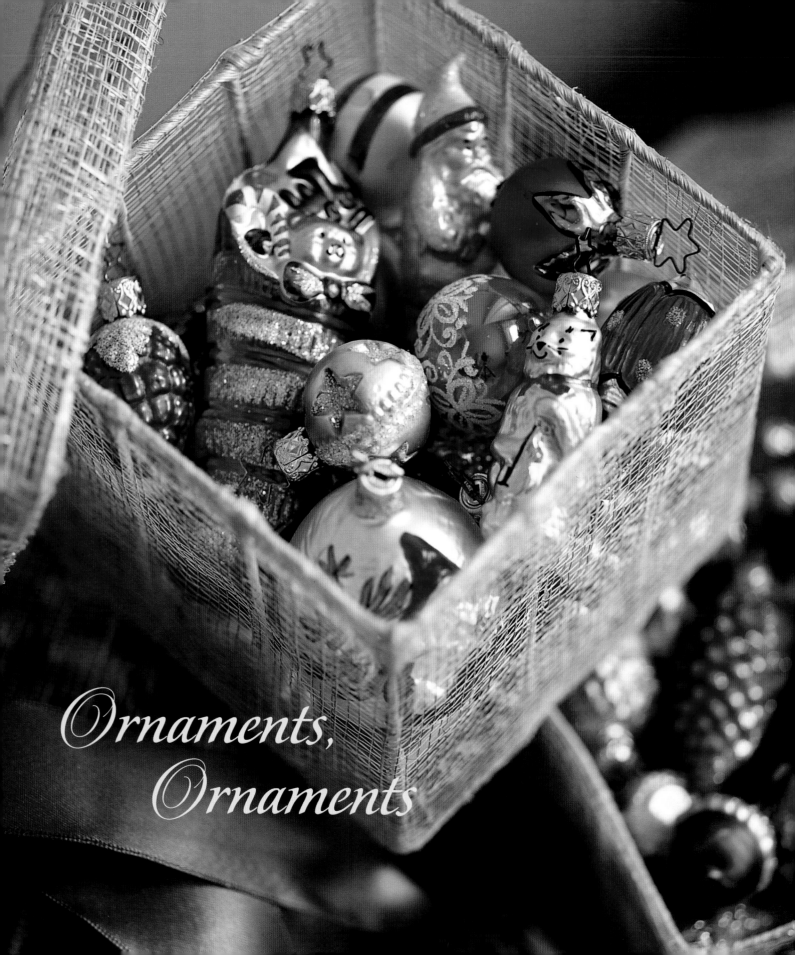

Ornaments, Ornaments

My Glittering Prizes

I bet you won't be surprised to learn that my collection

of Christmas ornaments grows every year. Not since

I was a teenager have I been able to hang each

and every one on the tree. My husband, Dan, tells me

I have more decorations than would fit on the tree at

Rockefeller Center. So I display them in bowls and

boxes, on mantels and sideboards and dressers. They're

peeking out from bookshelves, light fixtures, kitchen

cupboards. They're still waiting to surprise me.

Why have ornaments if you can't put them all out for the holidays? I like to create little stories with mine. I'll start off with a random bunch and pick and choose, replace and rearrange, until a theme begins to emerge. For a fanciful composition, I inverted one of those modern mesh Christmas trees and filled the resulting cone with a bouquet of ornaments; in the end, I wired the ornaments together for stability. Over the years, I've collected tree toppers. Luckily, these spires look great in glass, especially slender stemware and crystal candlesticks. Clustered together in front of a mirror, they appear to double in number and suggest the turrets of a shimmering fairy-tale castle.

Think outside the box, even if that means inside a container.

The Christmas season doesn't replace everyday life; it's a bonus. Don't banish your usual touchstones, but instead look for ways they can star in the holiday scene. Every time I pass my Limoges-inspired compote I admire it, so at Christmas I definitely want it to be part of the party. Here it has

Everyday objects deserve to dress up for the holidays too.

been overloaded with ornaments tucked into a pillow of moss, with a glamorous satin ribbon trailing down. Suddenly it's transformed into an accessory that looks as if it were made expressly for a Christmas tableau. Leaning the lid alongside the compote gives a lift of energy to the scene, as if all those decorations had pushed the top right off.

upon a pedestal

1   2

Forget the traditional formulas for pairing objects. Go ahead and make your own rules.

Who says candelabra must hold tapers? Instead, dress candle bases with glass ornaments to create an indoor holiday *gazing* ball. On another day, top the candleholders with gilded walnuts or fresh *fruits*. Candle glue will hold everything in place.

Glass ornaments sparkle with holiday glitz beside a formal silver compote, mixing in enough fun to keep the scene *lively*. Don't be afraid to pair gold with silver; cast iron with bronze. I think all *metals* coordinate.

For Christmas, my cement-face wall pocket wears a crown of *shimmering* bubbles atop a coiffure of eucalyptus and cedar. Dan calls this "Bacchus meets Dickens's *Ghost* of Christmas Past."

3

A
big lift

Tall ceilings can be a double-edged sword at Christmas. Their soaring height suggests a magnificent Tannenbaum — but it's pretty darned hard to maneuver a ceiling-high evergreen and secure it in one of those thumbscrew stands. My advice (as one who's been there) is a shorter tree on a table; set it in an urn for a powerful vertical presence.

- ✣ Wedge the tree into a bucket of wet sand that's been fitted inside a heavy urn. A few bricks will come in handy for ballast, if it's needed. Keep the sand wet and the tree will stay fairly fresh.

- ✣ For a lush look, lay a full wreath across the top of the urn before you put the tree in.

- ✣ Make short work of decorating with oversize ornaments and trimmings — big stockings, full-figure dolls, giant stars, great glass ornaments.

- ✣ I couldn't get over the effect of the outsize ornaments, so I stuck a fairy doll on the porch wreath, instead of a ribbon.

Some of my favorite ornaments are outright opulent, in luscious silvers and purples that are about as dressy as anything I have at home. A little goes a long way, but to play off the effect of the lush metallics, I'll pull pieces of gold-edged china from the kitchen and fill them with naturals. The pinecones I pick up along my street are from different neighbors' trees, so they vary in size. I spray them gold and silver randomly, then toss in a few metallic walnuts. As a focal point, I reach for a topiary ball — gold leaves glued to a Styrofoam ball.

*Silver and gold, from leaves to pinecones,
work as a contrast in textures.*

hen setting out shiny glass ornaments, think about how they will catch the light. During the day, sun streaming into rooms interacts with decorations in an ever-changing spectrum. Fair weather or foul, the midday glow will become the long shadows of late afternoon. At night,

Light is the crowning dimension in a display of ornaments.

ornaments near flickering candles, twinkling tree lights, or a tabletop lamp will beckon merrily. Old-fashioned glass salt cellars, back in vogue after being virtually unknown to an entire generation, can do more than hold seasoning. Here, they are makeshift pedestals that unify gold glass globes.

An ornament
holds all the loveliness of
Christmas, in miniature.

My mom tells me that when I was a toddler one of the very first objects to enchant me was a Christmas ornament. Of course I had no idea of its great meaning; I adored its sparkle and I loved its glitter. I know now that an ornament is a symbol of the season and a message of hope, a mirror of fashion or the cue to a family legend. Each one starts out as something created just to please the eye; that's what it is to visitors seeing your tree for the first time. But for you, who have hung that slightly chipped angel on the tree for years or remember the chubby little hands that created your goofy clay snowman, the most valuable ornaments go beyond loveliness, straight to the heart.

baubles

Woodland
Wonder

I *love a woodland theme*

at Christmas because it's so easy to build a mood of enchantment. Forest-inspired decor starts with natural ingredients — evergreen boughs, juniper and winterberries, grapevines, pinecones, even ordinary bare branches. Once these elements are combined with my everyday pieces, I'll toss in just a dash of gold and silver for sparkle. Prisms from old chandeliers, which I can't help thinking of as crystal snowflakes (pages 52–53), are some of my best ornaments. I love the fabulous way they reflect, refract, collect, and magnify the light from sunshine, Christmas tree bulbs, and candle flames.

What could be more at home in the forest than reindeer and rabbits? One Christmas season I borrowed a vintage mounted deerhead from a friend for our dining room. To give it some holiday whimsy (following page), I draped a wreath round its neck, then festooned the antlers with glass prisms suspended on pale silver ribbons that are a good foil for the room's navy walls. Spindly twig trees work best in numbers; here they stretch up to meet the navy walls, which stand in for the night sky. The lounging rabbit is from my Easter collection; with his dark clothing he's right at home in the winter woods. Meanwhile, the bronze deer, a modern copy of an antique, also slips into the winter forest mood (opposite). Deer are available now in so many materials — silver and gold plate, celluloid, ivorine, and fiberglass.

Silvered and gilded nuts, in fashion during the 1940s and 1950s, are finally popular again, but with a twenty-first-century spin: they're spray-painted. A glass trumpet vase holds an overflow of walnuts — some are gold and some silver — but you could also paint unshelled chestnuts, almonds, or hazelnuts. The twig trees are wrapped in scraps of burlap, a twist on traditional root-ball garb for live trees.

Magic in the Winter Forest

While I love to be snuggled indoors where it's warm,

the woods in winter have always charmed me.

On a snowy day in the midwest the woods are silent,

serene, safe. Decorations inspired by the forest

have a timeless style; they are inexpensive, colorful,

dramatic, fragrant — they're a natural. Bring some

of their magic into your home for the holidays.

A crowd of folks are more easily wined and dined in a buffet setting, but when I invite a few good friends for a sit-down meal, I love to create the most lavish, imaginative table possible. In fact, this woodsy scene is so elaborate that I resort to serving the courses in different spots. Early on we will have cocktails and hors d'oeuvres in the study, then dinner at the dining room table (opposite), and finally coffee and desserts at the server (left). Moving around gives us a chance to stretch our legs, and it gives me an opportunity to pull out all my decorating ideas.

Honeysuckle in the chandelier puts this woodland ambience over the top.

A woodsy table doesn't need "just-so" arrangements. I set out one favorite piece — a bronze deer to saunter across the Christmas landscape — then scatter gilded oak leaves, pinecones, and greenery amid the place settings. To me, this is more intriguing than a stiff, symmetrical centerpiece poised in the middle of the table. At each plate a golden glass pear ornament serves as both place-card easel and favor. My table settings may be quirky, but I've noticed that they encourage guests to feel more relaxed and convivial, an appealing effect at the holidays.

Nature inspires the enchanted winter forest;
a tight schedule inspires its artful chaos.

naturally festive

1 2

Decorating with red doesn't have to be a Christmas cliché.

Ordinarily there are candles in the glass *sconces* above my fireplace. But at the holidays, I create a decorative *parfait* by layering apples, pears, pinecones, and ornaments. It's a *feast* for the eye.

Well, what did you think the partridge did with that fruit from the tree? A *perfect* red pear cradled in a nest is a lovely *surprise*. Just behind it, bright red cranberries fill a crystal vase.

Here's my *refinement* of the commercial food basket — it has something for now, something for later, and something for *memories*. Fresh fruits mingle with compatible ornaments in a lidded basket that will be on hand for years to come.

If you are as crazy about Christmas trees as I am, why not have more than one? The dining room deserves to feature its own tree for diners to enjoy. This graceful beauty is perfectly proportioned to stand in a tall, double-handled urn. To go along with the woodland motif, vines and bunches of preserved pepperberries are natural accents amid the clear- and colored-glass ornaments. Strings of white fairy lights look like that many stars in the sky. I didn't want a topper on the tree, so in its place we created the most outrageous bow ever seen in Kansas. My holiday presents for the evening's guests are ready and waiting right there, under the tree.

Bring the essence of Christmas — an evergreen — into your dining room.

 To keep guests happy and steer traffic flow away from the busy kitchen, I put together a drinks station in our study. Positioned on a narrow drop-leaf table, the bar succeeds because it works on different levels: a compote holds ice; a plateau offers glasses, and a platter accommodates

The drinks station goes woodsy for Christmas cocktails.

decanters of spirits. A stately land-scape charger fills out the scene. My Wisconsin friends tell me that tree top-pers like the ones on the table are par-ticularly popular back in their state. It seems growers there trim and shape Christmas trees extensively and sell the trimmed tops as table decorations. I've packed mine into an urn and a silver chalice.

$\mathcal{A}$ new
teatime
venue

For holiday tea, I invite friends to step into my entry. I realized one Christmas that the entry is perfect for casual daytime entertaining. It's flooded with afternoon sun and furnished with comfortable, cushiony chairs. I prepared almost everything ahead of time so that I actually got to enjoy my own party!

- ❧ A hall table and wirework tray on a wrought-iron tea table are conveniently located at the foot of the stairs, away from traffic flow. Serving at different levels encourages everyone to mingle.

- ❧ Wreaths and garlands on the windows limit decorations to the perimeter of the space, making the most of the area while keeping the smallish space totally usable.

- ❧ My one grand gesture? A garden fairy comes indoors to be the guardian angel of the tea service. The fairy dust in her saucer is really granulated sugar.

- ❧ Because the entry opens onto other rooms, guests feel free to wander about to see all my other holiday decorations.

Garlands, looped around doorways and rooms, are like evergreen exclamation points.

I adore garlands: big, blowsy, boisterous garlands. The sedate swag, hung primly from symmetrical hooks—well, it bores me. I want my garlands to look as if they've just rushed in from the forest and danced themselves into position. I mix lengths of evergreen, all different kinds of them, with grape-vines. Then I drape them throughout the house, around cornices, above doorways, and along window frames; I hang them on headboards and sideboards. Garlands look wonderful wrapped over themselves, perhaps with a focal point at their center, like the leaping reindeer that's attached to one of the evergreen dervishes you'll spot in my dining room.

boughs

Illuminations

The Holiday
of Lights

Light brings everything together. A room, though it

may be filled with flowers, ornaments, and other

decorations, comes to life only when lights glow. Winter

sun yearns for lamps to burn brightly. During the

holidays, I toss out the notion that candles should

be lighted only after dark; I want candlelight reflected in

ornaments, glass, mirrors, and silver — in all my rooms.

Consider the ceiling fixture. Its holiday decorating potential is awesome yet often overlooked. Any ceiling light has the makings of a centerpiece; it has an architectural foundation that all but guarantees decorations will hang where they won't be touched. Creating a symphony of ribbons, ornaments, greens, and branches is less daunting than constructing a conventional centerpiece; after all, gravity is on your side. What are the rules? I can tell you that beyond honoring proportion, there are none. An eloquent example is the fixture above my friend Merrilee's dining table (opposite); traditional prisms mingle with magnifying glasses suspended from tasseled cords. In my study (left), pussy willow and pinecone ornaments accompany gold balls and sheaves of winter wheat.

Points of light

Lamps, whether they're set on tables, mounted on walls, or standing on the floor, deserve their rightful share of holiday attire. Once they've been primped and pampered, you'll never overlook them again.

- ❧ Matching candlestick lamps need little more than sprigs of greenery and quickly tied bows. So that they don't look too symmetrical, one lamp's bow is tied high and the other low.

- ❧ "Countless" is a word that's often overused, but in terms of decorating lampshades, it's an understatement. One of my favorite treatments is stitching on glass ornaments. After the holidays, just snip the thread and remove the glass balls.

- ❧ A mirror behind or below any light, whether it's electric or candle, will intensify the effect of the light. Conversely, lights in front of daylit windows will tend to disappear.

- ❧ Consider how lamps and candles will look from out of doors, through windows at the front of the house. Rooms saturated with light appear more harmonious from outside.

You don't need a lot of detail to hint at a greater picture: this tableau is essentially simple, but it effectively conveys the peace and tranquility of the night forest. Set in a rusty urn, a lone moss topiary suggests the woods; a few crystal prisms could be scattered

Let it glow, let it glow, let it glow.

about as stars or snowflakes. The mirror in the background instantly doubles the effect of the tree and its own corsage of twigs and berries; it sends the flames of the candles dancing like moonlight on a lake. Just as no two elements in nature are identical, the candles stand in slender, mismatched glass sticks.

The glow of candles is such a colossal part of the holiday. Through the season, I'll set candles about the house, wherever my eye falls. Still, even I didn't realize how much candles contributed to the holiday until the year I noticed they'd got their own category in my Christmas to-do list. It's instant gratification to find a spot that's been overlooked and plop a candle (or a dozen of them!) there. I put them on candleholders, but also on pedestals, trays, cake stands, flower pots. Urns make wonderful candle-holders; a little bit of sphagnum moss completes the look. On their wonderful porch, Merrilee and Mike Bozzoli light dozens of candles to twinkle and glow. They've placed them in lanterns and glass candelarias; they set candles on tables, in windows, on the porch floor, along the railing. Candles — so simple, so beautiful, so Christmas.

candelabracadabra

Candles will glow
where they're planted.

Randomly anchor a few kitchen
candles in a deep bowl filled with
unshelled nuts. Vintage glass
ornaments, which have their own
patina from time, will
reflect the candles' *glimmer*.

For a grouping *rich* in texture,
arrange birch-wrapped candles in a
woven basket with ornaments and
tassels. Place a small plate or
tray inside the basket as a base to
hold the *pillars* steady.

Tea lights with stature, here from
vintage nut servers, reflect on a
glossy surface. Glass ornaments
bubble and glint around the edges of
the little dishes. This display
works well on a highly *polished*
table or the mantel.

2

3

A spirit glows on winter's darkest days.

Our homes are lit with incandescent, fluorescent, and halogen lightbulbs. We've got central heating, too. But candles and fireplaces are essential to our spirit as well as our comfort. Candlelight turns dinner into romance; it erases care from our faces and bathes us in its glow. The blazing hearth is companionable and cozy—even when it's a cinch just to turn up the thermostat. At Christmas especially, I crave these symbols of hope and warmth. I believe that they carry the promise of the new year and joy still to come. A Christmas without candles would be unthinkable. A cold hearth in December would be unbearable.

candles

Settings for Guests

*L*oosen up and rethink the way

you set the table for holiday meals. Custom may dictate matched dinnerware arranged according to some rigid formula — I think that's so dull. A well-set table is one that delights guests, sparks conversation, and reflects the host's personality. Scale and color are the yin and yang of table decorating. One evening I'll have the table reach for the stars, with pedestals of ornaments, pyramids of fruit, lofty candelabra, and arching statues. For a breakfast, it may be low, low, low — fruits scattered about right on the bare table, pure white porcelain, pure white napkins.

I like to pluck table decorations from other rooms of the house. An unruly stack of books is a good stand for a mix of glass pinecones, some vintage ornaments, and real pears coupled with stone ones. I repeat the combinations down the center of the table, but no two are identical. Another one of my favorite table tactics is to recruit serving pieces for offbeat uses. Let a big teapot hold the forks, spoons, and knives for a buffet (pages 98-99). Go ahead and fit your silver candlesticks with glass ornaments. You can still have candles on the table. Just put some tea lights out; let them twinkle from delicate sherbet dishes.

Do you get tired of red and green? By the middle of December, I could easily banish both from my tables. My Christmas palette generally tends toward golds and silvers, whites and creams, even blues and pinks. What really matters is the fun of the table; when it's like a living board game, I feel I've accomplished something. If I can sneak in a visual pun or two — like the partridge plate and pear table tableau (page 92) — my guests will pick up the spirit of Christmas.

Christmas Day at the Table

My favorite meals of the entire holiday season are

on Christmas day. Like yours, my shopping is finished

(both the work of my shops and the presents I've

bought to give). The gifts have been wrapped, the food

has been organized, the family is about to arrive.

My home is ready; really, it's never looked more

beautiful. I look forward to the hours ahead, at home,

enjoying time with family. And there are

always a few surprises.

An inviting table tells my guests how glad I am that we're together. But palatial formality is not part of my vernacular. I want everyone to feel comfortable and relaxed. I love the rustic look of a twig runner on a fine linen cloth, especially when it contrasts with the table's more predictable silver and stemware and some Majolica chargers. At each place setting I leave a favor, a little wrapped gift that's been topped with a family of bottlebrush trees. Inside, each diner will find something I've slipped into a pretty frame. My flea-market buddy Marsee will get a photo of us wrestling home summer's best market find; Cheryl the restaurateur will open a postcard of the hotel where we stayed on our dining trip to New York; Dan will have a little saying of his that I asked a calligrapher to write out: "But, Mary Carol, what in the world would you do with that?"

setting layers

Like the bow on a present, a pretty napkin ring heightens anticipation.

Casual, say hello to Classic: Seeded eucalyptus tucked into a silver *snowflake* napkin ring surrounds a diagonally rolled, sage-striped napkin — a *perfect* presentation for lunch.

Milliners know a good thing when they see it, and they work with so many items that can be designed into napkin rings. Here, a trio of gold berries is wired to a *vintage* glass ornament.

A friend once told me that the only good *ribbon* is a double-face ribbon, and she comes awfully close to being *right*. A luscious café au lait satin band is the *halo* for a miniature Madonna portrait.

1

A good serving table is hard-working, but it's also entertainment for diners as they consider what they'll have to eat and drink. This one was inspired by a single element: the ceramic topiary of shiny red apples arranged in an urn. I wanted to put out some glass ornaments anyway and this was a neat way of stacking them.

Come one, come all.

They're piled into glass cloches that were inverted to be filled, then righted on the table. The cloches are different sizes, giving the arrangement the rhythm of a cityscape. To balance the crimson of the apples, the ornaments are all in shades of soft moss. Green is echoed in the chubby teapot that has been filled with inexpensive utility flatware. The plates are stacked, the wine chills, and candles glow.

Let visions dance in their heads

Blessed is the house with Christmas company. And when company spends the night, the celebration becomes that much more personal. You'll put out the good towels; you'll dress the bed in the most luxurious linens; and you'll definitely have a few Christmas hospitality tricks up your sleeve.

- Tie a stocking to the headboard. I always fill mine with evergreens for their glorious scent, but my favorite was the year I slipped a potted conifer right into the stocking.

- Replace artwork above the nightstand with a wreath. Even though we have lamps, a bedside candle is a treat. I like to wake to an old-fashioned clock on Christmas morning — forget LCD numerals!

- Improve the chocolate-on-the-pillow idea. Send a holiday guest to dreamland with a box of bliss: a good mystery book, a personal stereo, and a recording of Bach's Brandenburg Concertos.

- Make your milk and cookies say something. Present them under a glass cloche tied with a slip of ribbon; it's homey and it's luxe.

What is the color of Christmas?
It's whatever color you want it to be.

You may be surprised to learn that one of my favorite Christmas colors is

brown; brown kraft paper wraps tantalizing packages that come in the brown

delivery truck; the best Belgian chocolate is rich bittersweet brown; copper, a

light coffee brown, reminds me of lustrous ribbons and cheery jingle bells. Rose,

lavender, peach, blue, and so many other colors are right there on my holiday

palette. When I do decide to work with traditional red and green, I'm more

likely to look for shades such as sage green or deep burgundy. After all, nature

came up with so many colors; let's invite them all to the celebration!

color

Little Surprises

A Wink and a Nod

Think small. In the midst of the lavish gestures and

intricate schemes of the holidays, a quiet surprise

brings pleasure far greater than its effort. Tuck a tiny

boutonniere in a visitor's lapel; mail a beautifully

wrapped present to someone you see every day; bake the

blueberry pie that is your family's favorite.

I'm fond of bouquets of all kinds, especially ones that have trinkets; I also love little bouquets set where no one would expect to find them. On my Victorian folding screen, for example, I tied a porcelain creamer with pale green grosgrain ribbon; it's filled with a couple sprigs of boxwood and a string of beads. Another favorite makeshift vase is the hanging glass votive holder that I outfit with a pine branch rising from cranberries in water. Singly these elements are inconsequential; together, they're so charming.

Finish dressing your rooms with corsages of humor.

I love the way my friend Merrilee concentrates the Christmas decorations in her living-room on the mantel. It comes as a delightful surprise, since the first glimpse of the room as you enter leads you to conclude that the holidays have not yet arrived at her house. This pinpoint decorating is practical, too, as it leaves most of the room unfussy and comfortable for the everyday activities like perusing the newspaper, watching television, listening to music, sipping a drink. Merrilee's mantel has the Nell Hill's layered look, with garlands, ornaments, pictures, and mirrors all leaned up against each other to create a rich tableau. The greenery is purposely off-center — the section Merrilee let trail down one side injects movement.

When you're not inclined to start from scratch for an over-the-top holiday scene, just tweak the everyday elements of your rooms. A moss-green bow tied around an urn of feathers and cattails brings a holiday aura to an already dramatic arrangement. On her singular living room mantel, my pal Merrilee let me create another one of the puns my long-suffering friends know they will have to endure; this time it involves ornaments. What is it? It's ornaments on the scale — weighting for Christmas, waiting for Santa.

Look for quick ways to shift the everyday into holiday gear.

unstuffy stockings

1 2

For the best stockings, blend silly with sophisticated.

The jester's sock, designed by the staff at G. Diebolts, comes complete with button accents and a *curlicue* toe — an amusing contrast to the crewel fabric and fringed cuff. Perhaps you'd add a bell or a *seashell*.

An exaggerated boot-shaped stocking of formal *toile* hangs from a drawer pull. Coordinate the stocking fabric with your *upholstery* or curtains.

Welcome Santa with a stocking of elegant *champagne*-colored silk, its iridescence dotted with dozens of tiny *pearls* and banded with an opulent beaded trim.

Have you ever had the delicious experience of designing something unintentionally? While they were decorating their living-room mantel, my friends Donna and Tim Zimmer had nestled beaded ornaments in a blanket on their settee for safekeeping.

Offhand can be every bit as rewarding as orchestrated.

When the phone rang, Donna set the package she was holding — a ribbon-tied bundle of old volumes on its way to a book-loving friend — beside the ornaments. The effect was charming, mingling warm shades of copper and celadon in a timeworn patina. It wasn't a fastidious, deliberate Christmas display, and it wasn't going to remain for the duration of the season. It was serendipity, though.

All
present

Early in November, when pie-in-the-sky holiday fantasies frolic through my imagination, wrapping presents promises to be a pleasant, tranquil activity. By December, I'm desperate for time and I've run out of Scotch tape. My solutions:

❧ I skip the gift wrap. I'll tuck a special bottle of wine and four tumblers in an urn filled with moss and pine boughs.

❧ I look for packaging that's part of the gift. Baskets, pretty hatboxes, wooden crates, painted trays, even tart pans look terrific as they are.

❧ I learn from my customers. A Nell Hill's shopper may be delighted to discover a beautiful silver-handled walking stick and she'll also fall in love with a plaid lap blanket. Somehow the two items are perfect mates, and a cardboard box doesn't even enter the equation.

❧ I concentrate on fabulous ribbons, and add to the allure of bows with feathers, costume jewelry — anything that can be tied on.

When I do want a paper wrap for gifts, brown kraft paper is my choice. It's a starting point for all kinds of embellishments. Because it comes in long rolls, I don't have to piece together loose sheets of paper for bigger gifts. And I enjoy saving money when I'm not compromising on quality; who doesn't? I decorate packages with touches of nature, such as a ribbon-tied bundle of glittered sticks. Gold- or silver-sprayed nuts are stuck to the wrap with a dab of hot glue. I also like the simplicity of kraft paper with a formal toffee- and-pewter satin ribbon lattice. I've been a frustrated bow-tier for years, and I compensate in lots of ways. The neatly clipped ribbon ends are a good example.

My gift wrap of choice? Brown kraft paper.

From year to year my guiding light is simplicity.

Decorating that leaves you too tired to enjoy the season is not the point! Neither is the exquisitely wrapped package you're too tired to give, the personalized cards you're too tired to write, the succulent meal you're too tired to enjoy. You can give your family the simple joy of Christmas without sacrificing any of the season's splendor, gaiety, or reverence. Find the humor and beauty in the season and share them—this is the gift that multiplies each time it's given. Seize the romance, the fellowship, and the charity; give back to your community, your church, your school. Have a happy Christmas.

simplicity

Acknowledgments

This book owes its existence to countless talented people, all of whom were as dedicated to it as I am to my store. Smallwood & Stewart's team of Bruce Shostak, Alexis Siroc, Ella Stewart, and John Smallwood created this book, working along with Jean Lowe and her incredible staff—Polly Blair, Janice Carter, Delsie Chambon, Stephanie Farley, Becky Kanning, Elizabeth Nuelle, and Marti Petty—at Andrews McMeel Publishing in Kansas City. Writer Mary Caldwell got the words down, and photographer Bryan McCay captured the images.

Around the house and at special events, a few extra sets of helpful hands are always great, and I've been fortunate to have plenty of those. Some of the real troopers are Marsee Bates—who went without sleep for three days to make sure things were perfect for me; master gardeners Gloria Case and Linda Coulter; Connie LaRue always helps at a moment's notice; and Cheryl Hartell—whose food made the autograph party. Just because they're good people, Debbie Beagle, Carol Burns, Ricky Creamer, Melinda DiCarlo, Deann Dunn, Robin Enright, Brenda Graves, Jane Graves, Ann Humphries, and Nancy Neary all pitched in at key moments.

The Atchison Fruit Market, right here in my hometown, and Red Cedar Country Gardens, in Stillwell, KS, kept me in evergreens throughout the long, exhausting selling season. The warm atmosphere there, and the bottomless supply of festive greenery, made a sometimes-trying job a pure pleasure.

My sincerest appreciation goes to my dedicated day-to-day, full-time, rain-or-shine staff at Nell Hill's, who keep the wheels turning: Rani Bassi, Sue Bell, George Bilimek,

Wesley Calton, Suzy Clayton, Shirley Cline, Joe Domann, Carolyn Dunn, Judy Green, Dillon Kinsman, Nichole Liggett, Shannon Mize, Gloria Nash, Cheryl Owens, Adam Royer, Angela Stuebs, Kerri Wagner—and, of course, my right hand, Cyreesa Windsor.

Also, my invaluable part-timers: Emily Armstrong, Heather Brown, Katie Burns, Carolyn Campbell, Joan Carpenter, Chubby Darrenkamp, Cherrie Ehlert, Barbara Fricke, Delbert Gentry, Leslie Gwynn, Gail Hansen, Vicki Hinde, Jo Hines, Zachary Hoyt, Carey Huffman, Amber Kuhnert, Penny Linscott, Ardena Loch, June Lynn, Mallory Meyer, Evelyn Monea, Angela Mullins, Theresa Murphy, Lois Niemann, Sarah Nolting, Heather Owens, Jamie Servaes, John Shackleford, Corby Shields, Kathy Sledd, Gretchen Sullivan, Geri Weishaar, Marcellini Weishaar, Connie Wietharn, Lindsey Wietharn, Bill Wilson, and Laurie Wilson.

Thanks also to our many friends and customers, in Atchison and beyond, who make every season festive and who teach me so much every day. You're all terrific, and without you there would be no store to write about.

Finally, as always, I give my deepest thanks and love always to those dearest to my heart, Dan Garrity and Kelly Garrity.